Missing

Missing

Malcolm Povey

Smokestack Books
1 Lake Terrace, Grewelthorpe, Ripon HG4 3BU
e-mail: info@smokestack-books.co.uk
www.smokestack-books.co.uk

ISBN 978-0-9931490-9-2

Smokestack Books is represented
by Inpress Ltd

To Jackie and our children,
Daniel and Louise.

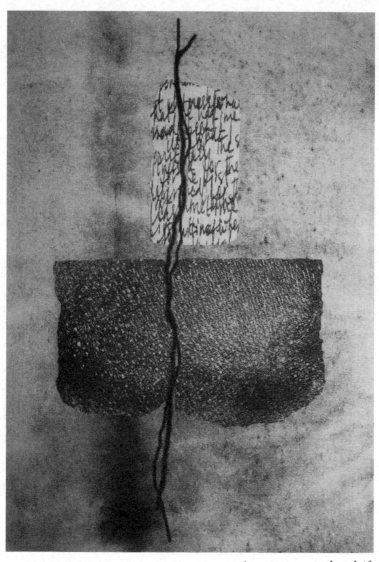

*An empty coracle adrift
on loss and loneliness.*

Contents

In the Store

Trying on a coat
you give a little –
I'm afraid a man's
vocabulary lacks the word –
'A little wriggle', let it be,
of your shoulder,
and look behind, and down,
to see, I guess, how it hangs,
and all our months of worry
fall away: your cancer;
its treatment; our daily
slither to oblivion.
I see the girl in you,
who hasn't gone, who lives
in laugh, and eye, and wriggle,
who lives.

Bedtime

'Do you know your jimjams
are round your ankles?' I ask,
sat on the crapper warmed
by your bum, then bend
and tug them up, over
your cancer-thin thighs.

'Love's young dream,' you giggle,
flanneling your face, one hand
gripping the rim of the sink,
and then, as you wobble,
'It's funny, the places
you end up'. Scanner.
Wig-shop. Near worn out.

'Yes,' I say, 'Life likes
to remind you how little
you matter.'

To life.

But not to me.

Inexpressible

Useless to try to describe
the touch on your chest
at dawn of the arm
of your wife may soon
be dead.

You wish it could last
for ever, but you're not a kid
and know it can't,
but love it.

Your Pre-set Breakfast

This cornflake box
is your castle
fights cancer;

this bowl, a moat
wards off death,
a breast
of life's milk;

this honey is hope
to boost blood.

You set them out
each night, a shrine
invoking up-and-about
tomorrow.

At the Limit

Who'd carry a book of poems
into hospital?

A place where useful work
is done, bone fixed,

babies birthed, cancer
conquered, and all

in a cheery voice
makes you feel, almost,

at home. But, when
baby is born dead,

cancer won't let go,
then, when science

tightens its lip,
and religion sidles up

to beg your soul,
it's time to seek

in verse, some word
for you, for it.

Little Brown Jobs

'Look at that,' I shout, 'Look!
The sparrows are back.'
A flock, first for a year,
scavenge the privet.

And you're back from chemo,
your future, like the sparrows',
fragile. Unwatched by God.

Little brown jobs!

We used to think them dull
but cancer makes you glad
for dull, the little brown days
that one day, for all of us,
just fly away.

The Last Flourish

How did I know, as December dusk deepened,
and the unseen robin sang loud song
to end the day it must have lived as spring,
the sky so clear of cloud, the leaves bright light,
that the last flourish was the last flourish?
For I knew, as my shoulders sagged,
'He won't sing again today,' and he didn't,
while I listened intent to absent song
and the darkness grew.

Thankyou Verse

It's easy to praise nurses,
like this girl of gentle touch,
soft voice, trained to persuade you
you won't die. Not now.
Not here, in this plastic
piss-wipeable chair,
as she hooks you up
to your evasively
abbreviated 'chemo'.

And even easier to curse poets
who, when not high on the sun
which they aren't often, brood
down in the clay with cadaver.

Just one of them speaks true.
And not the one
with the old-fashioned watch
hung upside down
on her untouchable bosom,
measuring the drip-drip-drip
of poison.

Day Ward

These, who take your bloods
and fasten you to shiny bags
of cancer-fighting fluid,
who do not seem to fear
that they will end up here,
sitting in this sweaty, plastic chair
where dozens of dying have sat,
while someone bustles round them,
talking of last night's tele,
pretending that they look well,
despite tube in arm, fear in eye,
these are the really useful.

They seem not to need to write,
or paint. To delineate what
has already been delineated
by far better than them. And if
they have affairs it's for the thrill,
not to spark off art. Or is it just
that aching feet dull the heart?
Or that the mind lies easiest
in young flesh oblivious
to surrounding pain?

After Chemo

My head on your cancer-thin thighs,
your fingers tickling my scalp,
'You've still got curls at the side,'
you say, and tug one, gently.

So late in life to notice.
All those each-other-neglecting
years, the cells did whatever
they do to spread cancer
through your bones.
Spread it now as we touch.

Never again the casual,
'How d'you feel today?'
while filling the kettle.
Each day a courtly circling.

While we wait, politely,
the barbarian storms on,
ebullient in your scan.

Laughs

You take off your wig,
your crown white and shiney,
to ask if there's any hair left,
back of your skull.

'Yes,' I say, stroking chemo-thin
tufts sticking out of your head.

'I look like Emu,' you frown,
staring, lashless, into the mirror.

'You look lovely,' I say, 'Why not
shave the last bits off? Ditch
the wig. Go boldly bald.'

'I'd look like Nosferatu.'

You tug your pointed ears wide,
and we explode in laughter,
laughter too scared for tears.

Radiotherapy

'Palliative' appals to pallor
with its hint of 'pall'.
What a thump to the heart
to read 'palliative' on your guide
to bombardment by X-ray cannon.

We are on the last lap
but neither timer nor timed
know its duration. There will,
no doubt, be terrifying corners
and desperate application of brakes.

I read 'palliative' and shake,
then take your arm, and hide
behind a caring, careless grin.

Failing

The mouse on the lawn
does not run away when I charge out
to throw a not-thrown ball at it.
It's dying. Too far gone to lift
its head or frisk its tail.

Upstairs, you're curled on the bed,
reluctant to rise to watch TV.
Too tired, after another balls-up
by the nurse, to grasp the hand
of routine and pretend things less bad
than cancer soon to win.

And I, the analogy-seeker, drink
another glass of red and lie to myself
about peaceful death, knowing
it just as likely enormous hurt
clubs you and mouse into submission.

Dying

You were always kind to the doctors:
direct gaze, smile to put them at ease
as they listed your cancer's advance.

Until, near your death, the doctor said,
'You're looking anxious, Jackie,'
and you levelled your still-lovely eyes
at him, your gentle voice, and said,
'Why shouldn't I, doctor? Every time
I see you, it's worse news.'

He winced and looked down.
Then fulfilled your prophecy,
announcing cancer in your eye.

Faith

Wouldn't it be nice to think that ah,
somewhere, with bright wings,
the Holy Ghost kindles our love
to fuel your fight with cancer?

Or, we could pose heroic. Rail
against the bearded oldie canes you
with disease because you stopped
telling your beads forty years ago.

But it's hard to believe even
a cruel, infinitely inventive God
would mutate your breast cancer,
and, having riddled your bones with it,
pop it neatly into your lachrymal gland.

Gaze

Your eyes stayed loving,
candid, but scared,
until the surgeon
slid his knife
past ball, to sample
cancer frolicking
in your gland.

He caused you pain,
pointless, professional
pain, because anyone
who looked at you,
tottering on stick legs,
or heard your gasping
speech, could tell
you were soon to die.

Yet still he cut
through your eye,
leaving a huge bruise,
and you, looking at me,
half-boxer, half-gazelle,
but terrified
of the next blow.

Closer

I grasp you in my arms
in anxious parody
of past embrace.

You gasp. I squeeze.
Endear. You gulp,
gasp again. The pill
won't go down.

Before too long,
unerotic,
you will.

And it will be
forever.

At the Garden Centre

Our last trip out.
Of course, we didn't know it.
You wanted a plant to paint.

Instead of a stick,
you leant on the trolley.
Wouldn't let me steer.

Annoyingly slow,
we crept around the displays,
bought a bright orchid.

Next day you fell,
before I was awake,
on the bottom stair.

Ten days later,
you were dead.

Transformation

In dying, your eyes
went topaz. Topaz,
dark-lit. I kept
looking in, hoping
for a loving light.

Your last words were
'I want to die, Malcolm.
I really just want to die.'
It hurt. But I think
you were trying to release me,
to turn inward the terrible
concentration of your eye
to watch your body unravel,
and release me, your tearful,
bald love, help me
to kiss you goodbye.

Which I did.

And will never do again.

Last Word

My love, at the last,
you lifted your arm,
your withered, loving arm,
and whispered, 'Mummy'.

You were lifted alright;
lifted right out of life;
lifted clear out of sight,
for ever. And ever.

Beads

While you were inside church
telling your beads, your sins,
I was outside, fuming at God
for wasting our kissing time
and fuming at you for falling
for stories spun by men
in dresses. New lovers,
with only Sunday to meet,
yet still you went to Mass.

God was jealous of you,
and I was jealous of God.
What did he have, I didn't?
The promise of eternal life,
I guess. Keep telling those beads,
gal, and you can have forever
and forever to sing my praise.
No egotist then, that guy.

That was when I had hair.
And you still had two breasts.

But near your last, your faith
long exorcised by reason
and your giggling love of life,
you turned down a neighbour's
offer of a parting prayer,
with a firmly spoken, 'No,'
the only word you spoke
that day. No beads in hand,
no Virgin lurking to seize
your departing soul, just you,
dying, and your earthly loves
gathered, crying, the beads
of tears their heart's true prayer.

Rock Postures

When we went to see Bobby D,
you said, 'Look at his thin,
stiff legs.' You loved them.

We laughed about them over
and over again, thin,
stiff legs of a rock genius.

Then cancer seized the stage:
your lovely legs shrank
to skin, string, and bone.

We would have lived with that,
but spine, brain, liver,
your life, your vivid, only you,

succumbed. No rock postures:
just my loveliest, carried out
in a body-bag, bumping walls.

Questions

My love, relentlessly,
you left me, whispering,
'I want to die, Malcolm,
I really just want to die.'

Did cancer and chemo
poison you to hate?
Did you want to free
me from survivor-guilt?

Or could you feel your body
packing up, despite years
of steering it through life,
so you abandoned ship?

Don't know. Don't know
the point of verse, of you
shrunk to a lifted arm,
a whispered 'Mummy',

a pronoun in a poem.

What's Frightening?

At first, entering rooms,
I feared your ghost,
sat on the settee
or flat in bed.

Though why I feared a shade
of you, who had always
done the best for me,
I do not know.

In just a day or two,
I've learned it's not ghosts
to fear, but the enormous
emptiness of rooms
without you,

their utterly silent,
utterly indifferent
stance to who comes in,
or who is carried out.

Silences

'I can't bear to think,' you cried
one night, grabbing my arm,
'Of you, sat alone at night,
on the settee, on your own.'

Mere days after your death,
I've learned I'd rather sit
on my own, less lonely,
less heart-hurting, than to sit
and listen to people who claimed,
once, to love you,
but never mention your name.

Gone

You, who I have addressed as you
in so many poems, for so many years,
are no longer you. You're all
used up. You're as empty as a politician's
kiss. Breathless as the corpse
you soon won't be. This longest day of the year,
I wish you'd walk back in, rolling the moon
like a hoop, or grasping it like a child
you'll not let out for fear of its extinction.
Writing to you is useless? It's all that's left to do.

Looking Back

There was a last time we walked the shore
and laughed in the cliff lift and exclaimed
at lizards lounging on hot stone.

But we didn't know it was the last:
neither savoured it nor sighed.

There was your last breath. I witnessed that:
your almost rabbit pucker, tiny exhalation,
leaving me to live, a starving fox,
ghosting beside a dying sea.

In the Photo

You stand, side-on to the camera,
shoulder hunched in your grey
dressing gown, scarf hiding
your chemo-bald head,
the kettle on, the tennis balls
I throw at squirrels by the tiles,
your dear, departed to bone
and rot and dust, hand, clenched,
as you stare into your death,
utterly alone, despite my love.

Naming your Eyes

'Hazel,' they might be called,
some shade between 'green'
and 'brown' for your eyes.

Neither pic nor memory
prompt. Love, I remember,
and laughter, shining,

and, at your death,
a small slit, a gathering
of moisture not a tear.

Courage

I

'Courage, mon brave,'
I joked, bad-accent,
to you, French teacher,
recalling *The Eagle*,
its stern-chinned heroes
strutting their stuff
in 'Luck of the Legion'.

'Courage, mon brave,'
as you fought cancer
and its cells stormed
your fort, over-running
all the plucky little fuckers
did their kepied best
to fight them off.

It didn't work. It
didn't work. You lie
in your grave. No-one
bubbles inanely,
'Courage, mon brave'.

You don't need it anymore.

II

'Courage' maybe
gets me out of bed? No.
I get out of bed because
I get out of bed, or bed
gets out of me. Who knows?
Who cares?

You're dead, my darling heart,
who needed no joke Frog
to stir you into fight.

Fight lost.

At your Grave

You can no longer love,
anyone, or anything. You did.
You made sure you told me,
our kids, our friends, that you did,
and you made art, though your hands
shook and you could barely stand.
'No-one will ever know how hard
this has been to do,' you said,
finishing your last picture.

I still hear your voice in my head,
but, when I kneel beside your grave,
clearing weeds, washing your plaque,
I know you can't love me, our kids,
or painting, any more. Not for anything
we've done, but because you're dead,
unable to care about the earth
above your skull, or my white, tearful
face looking down.

No-one Home

I come to this space.

It is the total absence
of you.

Your grave.

Where you are utterly gone.

I look at the farmer's field
beyond the fence

say, please,

send me a sign.

No-one does.

No-one ever will.

Resurrection

My little loveliness,
gone under ground,
gone far away
as way can be,
I talk to you
at night, late,
and say, 'You can't
hear me, I'm merely
reinforcing neural
networks,' then turn
to photo of your grave,
in hope to find
you rising thence,
to sit beside me,
laugh at this sad scrawl.

Cut Off

I never thought of you as amputee
though your breast was chopped off,
the left one, which I'd loved to cup,
cut off; your skin stretched thin,
on cobbled ribs, so that you couldn't
stand caresses there, never mind
passionate clutches.

Now, beyond embrace, an amputee
from you, I live alone.

Dazzler

When the fire-eater came through the door
of that Cairo café, and my four-year-old eyes
were dazzled by his flames, and dazzled
by their quenching down his throat,
was Cavafy sat there, sipping brandy,
remembering a youth who dazzled
his youth? I doubt it, though at your grave
today I was dazzled by the simple truth
of a life crushed, of a fine bobby-dazzler
reduced to patchy grass and a leafless tree.

No More

'Non e più,' you used to giggle,
on our halting, suburban walks,
or spotting a dead actor
when we cuddled, watching tele,
our Italian class helping us
to mock the cancer sneaking
through your bones.

'Benny Hill, non e più.'

'Last night's steak, non e più.'

'Our little dog, non e più.'

It covered everything,
even my long-lost hair:
whatever was chopped
and gone: 'My left breast,
non e più.'

It covers you, now,
and no laugh in that,
despite the laugh
you laughed, when you said,
barely able to walk,
to eat, almost dead,
after a hard-won joke,
'I can still make you laugh,
Malc, still make you laugh.'

You can't.

Hope

Waking from a dream of you,
I jump at a bump in the room.
Is it you? Back from the dead?
I peep, and just for the briefest
of brief blinks, think it is you,
but, as I focus, it's my shirt,
stripe-bright on the wardrobe door.

Another fucking Bank Holiday!
Another day of ghostless futility.

Despite

It comes back despite what it's seen;
the light that has looked down
on men buying women's mouths;
on babies never make it to toddlerdom;
the trench-dead and the trench-crippled.

It comes back. Every morning,
no matter how dark, the light
manages to say 'It's day, not night.'
How it does it, I haven't a clue.

Most mornings, I ignore it;
stay in bed with eyes closed;
watch my thin dreams dissolve
and cloudy thought form.

Who Laughs Last

You laughed at the sad singles
at a party where we, the only couple,
whispered 'No-one wants to talk to us.
Once they know we're married,
they make their excuses and scurry
back to the hunt.'

Now the bad joke is on us.
Sad singles indeed. You, single
in your grave; me, single-shopping;
single-supping; single-sleeping;
longing for you, in single combat
with futility.

Good Samaritans

You know those two Christians
live up the road?

They didn't attend your funeral.
They've never knocked on the door
to see how I'm coping,
because, I guess, we declined,
the day nurse said you were dying,
their offer of prayer.

And yet, when the woman
was done for drunk-driving,
you were the only friend
supported her at court.
Not one of her Christian crew
held out a hand.

They've just walked past:
eyes glued to the ground.

Jesus, Jackie, I'm Barracked

Jesus, Jackie, I'm barracked
by advice from naggers
who've never lost their love.

'Do a course. Teach a course.
Take a hol. Try net-dating.'

'Why,' I reply, 'take hol,
go hundreds of miles
to sit alone by a pool
when I can sit alone at home?'

Compassion instructs me:
they don't know what crap they talk.

No-one who 'advises' me, in lists,
or jocular-avuncular, has lost
their love. None have sat alone
in an empty room once shared with one
who was their life, who stroked their head
and said, near her death, the cancer
tearing through her bones, 'I love
every inch of your body'.

I knew it wasn't strictly true,
but the saying was love,
and the receiving, love.
Which neither death
nor stupid talk, can kill.

Illumination

I wake on your side of the bed
where you so lightly lay,
even when newly dead,
and, thinking of you,
smile, it seems, your smile,
and, just for a moment,
feel as you might have felt
when, still half-asleep,
I slipped my arm around you
and our skins became one.

Paying the Price

By accident, I clatter the watch
you bought me after I admired
its time-tidying face. I told you off
for wasting cash. Straightening
the strap, I can't straighten the past,
nor put away my pettiness.

No-one, you dead, will ever again
want to surprise me with such a gift
to brighten an otherwise chill,
non-celebratory day.
Or be much bothered – 'Ignore
the old fart' - if I turn nasty.

No way now to kiss and make up,
to bury won't-be-silenced truth
insists, no matter how we tidy time,
our acts of petty hurt endure
as long as good and kind. Though left
off epitaphs, they cut into our lives.

Memento

I used to tut at your habit
of buying multiple postcards
at every gallery we visited.

Past pettiness does not fade
like postcards. It goads.

Please, forgive me,
now you're dead,
and send me a card
from where you've gone.
Just one.

'Wish you were here,'
might help.

Losing

Losing your wife is not
like losing a fiver.

You cannot ask a teller
to refund her, no matter

how vivid their tale:
you cannot shrug, and say

I'll have another, then swig
and swagger hurt away.

The world becomes a mint
prints sorrow, night and day;

you cannot suck it clean:
it's always on your tongue.

I flip this scrap I scribble on
to find a blurry print-out

of a fragment of her face;
the dearest face, time has torn

up and thrown away
like a drunken gambler

tearing up his notes
to boast his win. Like him,

I have fivers aplenty
but none bear a promise

to give me back my wife.

'Once and Once Only'

Eating that poxy lunch,
while cancer ate you,
bullet peas, brick-filled mash,
thin drivel of mince,
drove us to leave and walk
the panto-postered town.

To live that again! To smile
at you. To hold your hand
leaving. Grimace at poor
mugs queuing up. To live
that again. Together.

Call Not the Kettle

You laughed when I called a colleague
'A clod-hopper'. 'That's such a brilliant word,'
you laughed. 'Clod-hopper. Hopper
of clods.' Now, you can't hop, jump clod,
nor live again your one-legged, giggling
hop into our bed the night, I believe,
our children were conceived. And me,
I'm the clumsy hopper hops thick clods of loss,
tripping, stumbling, sometimes laughing
in an antic, rural, clod-hopping sort of way.

Your Once Firm Signature

You started to sign your artwork **JP** when your hands were too shaky to write 'Jacqueline Povey'. I have a piece of paper where you practised **JP** several times beneath unravelling versions of your once firm signature. Unbearable as it is to think of how weak and ill you were when compelled to practise those initials, **J** is now my favourite letter. It gives me a little jolt of strength whenever I write it, charged with admiration and love for you. It reminds me you were my anchor and, just for that moment, writing **J** anchors me again. Even when my hand shakes and my eyes blur with tears.

Your Handmade Cards

'Jacqueline Povey'
was too long
for your shakey,
dying hand.

'JP' you adopted
instead. No justice,
of course; no peace;
and though its sternly
clear on a card or two
mostly it wobbles,
blurs,

down in the corner
of each hand-made print,
as your death
draws near, and, towards
your end, you sometimes
forgot it, leaving some
Christmas cards
blank.

And a blank Christmas
it was for us;
who could still say
'Jackie,' 'Jackie,'

though you were shrunk
to less than the wobble
in the final letters
in the final, hard-worked
card.

Widower

You sit alone
with what's left
of yourself,
the drinking habit,
the reading habit,
the habit of missing
your dead wife,
the habit of missing
her lovely habits –
but sitting alone
is not yet a habit;
waking alone
is not yet a habit;
not touching, or being
touched, is not yet
a habit.

They may become
habitual; if so you
will have shrunk
yet more. Shrunk
almost to nothing,
except the sense that
once there was more
to you and life,
though you cannot
name it and will have
forgotten your wife.

Advice

'Don't bear grudges,' I hear you say,
'Bitterness corrodes. Forgive
the friends who never phoned,
or visited, in the lonely months
I was dying. Those doctors
who sometimes made things much worse,
who unnecessarily knifed
my eye when anyone's quick glance
could tell death would soon
be shutting out the light. Who
were all for battering me
with radiation, despite me being
a stumbling skeleton. Forgive
yourself, for sometimes snapping
at me for walking slow. Forgive me,
for dying, for leaving you alone,
a broken column jutting out
of desert sand. Forgive everyone
and everything. Even cancer cells
which never ask to be born,
know no better than to kill.'

You're right, even though in putting
these words in your dead mouth,
my pen's a knife to stab us living
with our guilt. And no-one is forgiven:
not doctor, me nor you.

Valentine's Day

One thing to look back on
with some pride, this day
of pink and lacey sentiment
and money blown on junk,
is telling the consultant
you were too weak to bear
X-ray torment. No point
in blasting your eye when,
so clear to any caring glance,
you were about to die.

16 Nov 09

This very day last year
we ate at our favourite
and I stared at your anxious face
hoping you would live.

Four weeks later,
you were dead.

Are dead.

Eating out seems as pointless
as wishing you were here,
though easier to stop.

Silent Wife

Gone, the years and years
of ending our evening meal
with me swivelling to the left
to make room for my legs,
to chat about the day, our kids,
the news, lit or chemo.

All gone; gone with the laborious walk
to the scarey ward; careful
counting of pills; holding hands –
round M&S; sliding into scanner;
watching telly – gone

and never ever, never ever,
to come back. Holding hands;
irritable 'hurry up'; annoyance
that you pricked the flaws
in my arguments so flawlessly,
and me the lecturer, pontificator.

Your going broke my bridge,
left me talking to you gone.
Stone pillar, gabbling
in time's flood.

Alone on Cold Mountain

I'm not, but alone
on our smart settee, sits
two or three, that you bought
just before you died,
I am. Alone as I could possibly
be, remembering your sudden tears
one night, 'I can't bear to think
of you sitting on your own,
night after night on the sofa
where we used to hold hands.'
You knew that I would drink.
Trail ink across emptiness.
I'll never see Cold Mountain,
but endure it everyday.

Retail

Stood in Boots,
trying to decide which blade
fitted my razor, a voice,
'Is it Malcolm?'

Yes. In some version
of our language game.

Then she asked,
'How's Jackie?'

Stood there, in my aging bulk,
(the lingo says it's mine,)
I said, 'I'm sorry. Can't wrap it up.
She's dead. Been dead two years.'

Did the narrative bit, manfully,
but then, when asked if I'd retired,
burst into tears, a bald, bulky bloke
in Boots, giving, as I say, someone says,
'The customers a laugh'.

Waking

Last night, we kissed and cuddled,
whispered and wandered
through exuberant touchscapes
of lush and loving us.

I woke thinking you beside me,
and turned to cuddle again.
The sheet was cold.
You, two years dead.

Is it good to dream
of what we were
when waking
only goads despair?

Finding

Nearly two years after your death
I still find the odd long hair
of yours. It no longer upsets.
I drop it into the pan, or bin.
Your hair was never that important.
But when you lost it, chemo-bald,
and cancer whittled your limbs to sticks,
your eyes stayed lovely, liquid
and full of light as a gazelle.
Now, you can't even gleam as ghost.
Though I saw you in a dream last night,
we squabbled. I woke in tears.

Since You Died

Remember Wilf, I mutter,
fighting self-pity.

He must have been about sixty,
tweed jacket neither hip, nor trad,
just saggy. A slight stutter,
when he told us, bumped into
in a café, doubled at night
as Lancaster's first disco,
that he'd lived his life alone.
'People moan about marriage,'
he said, 'but I think they lack
the guts to admit being happy.'

So now, I tell myself,
remember Wilf. I had
forty-three years with Jackie,
an improvised dance
to life's changing beat,
hands clasped against knocks,
hugging sudden joys,
till death barged in.

Remember Wilf,
his unpartnered life,
and think yourself lucky.

I was.

But luck, as it always does,
staggered out onto streets of loss.
And remembering Wilf,
who must also be dead,
jacket long gone from the Oxfam shop,
doesn't help.

Amazon

Even with only one breast,
you were the loveliest.

Even when my loving fingers,
scraped against your ribs
and scraping, made you wince,
you were the loveliest.

Even when, after saying such lovely
words to me, 'I love every inch
of your body,' you died,

even then, my love, even then.

Your Water-Jar

Here, your dead fingers gripped,
and now-discarded brushes
dipped, as you fought,
trembling, to leave a mark.

Your Late Painting

Silver diamond.
Grey sun.
A slashed breast
on a pot of birth.
It might be cancer,
or a flower, fades
behind the window.
What the writing says
I do not know.
Nor the picture.
But it speaks to me.

By Accident

My typo made
your painter's water-jar
your painjar.

Cancer did the same,
but, being boss,
felt no need
to write about it.

Side-Effects

Your little feet fattened,
under chemo, under cancer,
driving you to buy furry, leopard-
spotted slippers you'd never have touched
until your feet, swelled by oedema,
were too fat for fashion to shoe.

Still here, flopping on a chair
beneath the dresser shrines
your portrait, gaze so tender, true,
these slippers, stalwarts
in the astounding loss of you.

Anniversary

I wake in my kayak
of sheet, prow of feet
drifting the cold sea
of your vanishing.

First thoughts are ice.

Grief's glacier creaks
and creeps, wishing
it could warm and melt,
but a white bear
on the floe of my heart
fears death of loss,
to snooze in its fur
and wake content.

You, my darling seal,
whose face so warmed
my winter-world,
are drowned. I'll never
feel your touch again.

Retired, Bereft

From cliffs of Heidegger,
from bogs of bad essays,
chill wind in committee,
I come to cleaning sink,
bath and toilet, like
some Czech intellectual's
internal exile. Though it's
cancer has sundered me
from you and job and life.

These tasks that you once did
alone, only annoyed
when I forgot to rinse
the bath, or sink a turd,
help fill my lonely day,
pass time, stave off collapse,
and plant in me, surprisingly,
your Flemish love of clean
and pleasing to the eye.

In the Swim

Have leapt, a salmon,
your face fading,
at falls of loss.

Failed.

      Fell back,
savaged by bear
of loneliness,
of lost navigation,
nerve-map of stars
shredded,
supple muscle pulse
spastic; the joy
of being in the stream
of you

      ripped out.

Fading

I can't remember the feel
of your unsick, skater's thighs.

Instead, I flinch at how they
thinned to string and sticks,

then your calves fattened redly,
fat feet would not fit slippers.

Bemused, fearful, proud, you said,
'I used to have such slim legs'.

They strode once, white booted stars,
in a film of then New Uni.

Innocent days. Days I hadn't
touched your thighs. Nor been touched

by them. Days I didn't have
to picture your bones, thinning alone,

beneath the mud and leaves
of your woodland burial ground.

After Watching *Two-Lane Blacktop*

When the dust clears,
and car is in the ditch
the dead are OK:
the living have to find
the road, reason
to drive on.

Your Painting

From what deep wounds do souls combine?
From pain, entwine?

It is not light moves upon the dark,
but seething dark frictions light.

We met young, torn by family.
In time, our wounds fused.

Dying, you called us 'soulmates',
a cliché, your voice made beautiful,

although, like your painting, that beauty
was born of cancer's dark threat,

the soon-to-be loss of all you loved.
Just so our love was carefully built

from intuitions of a fractured line,
tonalities of loss. A belief that art

could heal, without forgetting
the black ground of its beauty.

Aftershock

On the balcony, clutching
a small bottle of beer
from the mini-bar,
my legs shook.
My God, I thought,
this beer, sipped once,
is strong.

Then, from the bed,
you called, 'Malcolm,
the water in my glass
is tilting from side
to side. I'm scared.'

In the street below
people began to group.
Some crying.

'It's an earthquake,'
I said. You asked
what to do. 'Nothing,'
I said, 'Just see
what happens.'

That was nearly
twenty years ago.

We survived,
with a lively tourist
tale to tell.

Now, there's no more 'we'.
I pick my way
through the rubble of my days.
Earth has swallowed you up.
I quake each day.
Can't blame the booze.

Fuck the tsunami.

I want you back.

April the First, 2011

Now I'm sixty-four you no longer love,
nor need, me. No longer stroke my bald head,
nor tut at over-cooked cod and tell me
to give myself more time.

Time! I've plenty of that.
Days are endless corridors with only stumbling feet,
red eyes, to traverse. And now, a third birthday
since you died.

Yesterday, I sat past midnight hoping
to pre-empt the pain of waking – lone
Birthday Boy – by not going to bed
till April struck. Fool. I woke, as every day,
to loss of you; an urge to hide in sleep; a third
birthday without your giggle, 'April Fool'.

Another loveless year ahead. No gift from you,
no handmade card, no kiss. My shoulders hunch,
head hangs heavy. I try to kid myself these lines
are a sort of gift; your memory a sort of kiss.

April Fool! Our Japanese tree hasn't toppled
onto the lawn, but you, most certainly, have gone.
Rotting now, beneath a bed of daffodils planted
to kid us there's some chance you're coming back.

Communion

Dead, you're still the person
I talk to most, tell my most troubled
thoughts, joke with, sometimes whine,
'No-one cares.' You're still the one
that sees most sides of me,
though you can neither hear
nor see. Nor speak. Not tell me
when I'm silly; not joke, nor tell
your cancer-fears; not tick me off
for being rude, nor praise, bright
eyed, my loving care of you.

Though Jesus said,
'Let the dead bury the dead,'
and I, half-dead, have buried you,
you're still the only person
I speak to every day.

Dialogue

'It's lonely,' I say, to you, in my head:
the tele crowd has ceased its sporting din,
a half-read novel sleeps upon my bed.
The dark is cocky, certain it will win
when light turns off never to turn on again.

Though summer still, I tuck my duvet tight.
A gust, chill thought, almost makes me shiver.
You'll never smile again – my happiest sight –
your sparkling humour calm my queasy liver,
and every night's too cold without your touch.

'Lonely,' you reply, for once, tonight,
'Today, you walked beside the wide, bright sea,
took care to cream against the savage light
and quite enjoyed your salmon-salad tea.
Lonely! Just try for once being me,

stretched out in utter dark, a dark
so dark you cannot even call it black,
no friend to chat to, no sky-striving lark
to marvel at, not even an itch, or slack
now-wanted fold to remind I once was flesh.

Lonely! You try lying alone out here,
indifferent to the sun and rain,
annoyed your lover blunts your loss with beer,
stuck where we'll never meet, ever again,
then write your daft poems no-one will read –

as if I could speak, left out here to rot,
except in the head of a lonely old sot.'

Hopeless

This hand will lie and rot near yours,
my love. Next week. Next year. Dull
decades hence. The plot is booked.
My bones will lie beneath six feet
of wormy earth, weed-battling grass,
next to what's left of what was you.

I hope my bones will creep closer
to yours. That we might, dead,
hold hands. Kiss, perhaps. Bang
lipless teeth. And with this image,
love, am sure we won't.

In my Dream

Last night we made love,
intent, absorbed, two scholars
just on the brink of solving
a long-dead language. Metaphor
can't catch it. Let's just say
that, waking in my lonely bed,
last night's learned review
of God-knows-what slipping off
the coverlet, (-let? what's that
when probably not at home?)
I realised my little room
will never again be everywhere,
and, God-knows-why, heard
you say, though four years dead, so clear,
of my tears at *The Grapes of Wrath*,
'And aren't you proud of yourself.
Your tears.' You never were a comfy
duvet. I have to get out of bed,
I'm not sure why, something to do with
thickening my skin, day by day,
to still your voice, forget your touch.
It's what they all expect: friends; family.
But, as long as I'm me, I'll hear you say,
when I showed you my draft of *Sedgemoor*,
though your paintings hung all over Poole,
'You've worked harder than me, Malc,'
in your clear, honest way, sunlight
cleansing my germs of doubt, though
only now it strikes, just how precise
your praise. You didn't say my poems
better than your pics, or, indeed,
if they were any good at all,
but you had your Dad's admiration
for hard work, for scratters, who, though
their efforts came to naught, scratted.

Giggle

At the wheel of your ultimate driving machine,
your son counting the milk-floats only he could see
flash past your snail-chariot, you'd giggle.

Always, even ticking off a class
for its English hostility to French,
as if Henry Five still ranted on the box
and the Dauphin plotted to seize Bournemouth pier,
or joking with the cancer-man
that his offer to match you with another sick
conscript to help you fight his chemical war,
was like a dating agency for the nearly dead,
you kept that girlish giggle,
your joy at life's absurdity,
though the gangster-hard nun
from Glasgow was right to praise you,
'Jackie has a backbone of steel,
pure steel.'

But steel can't stop the rush of metastatic cancer,
nor, despite what twerps cry, 'being positive'
unjam the clogged-up lanes of life,
and when, without a giggle,
you muttered, 'Stop tormenting me,'
my deathbed chat the torture, I knew
the girl, my dear, steely girl,
was gone, and only a frightened woman
was left, wanting to die, to get it over with,
though you still found love and battled breath
to whisper, 'I know you mean it
for the best, but please stop.'

So we sat dumb as your last days
passed and, without a giggle,
you refused the offered prayer
from Christ's soul-hogging milkman.

Comfort

You are, some say, 'at one with the universe,'
and offer it as comfort.

You were never at one with me for long –
that moment when Louise came in, aged eight,
and lifted the sheets, shouting delightedly,
'I've caught you at just the most exciting bit!' –
cuddling in bed before breakfast, not knowing
where one skin ends and the other begins –
mute and mutual glances at a daft remark –
but couples are rarely 'at one,' which, I guess,
is why we call them couples – 'copules', I sneer
when bitter – and, as for that, I'm rarely at one
with me, but that's a topic for another time –
is it? why not now?
You heard what you said!

For now, let's try to imagine it, try
to find a way of putting it – here goes -
'the universe, in its pitiful indifference,
despite cosmic reluctance to commit,
has taken you to its dark bosom ... '
except there is no 'you' to enfold, no 'one'
to be at one, only the whizz and wheeze
of atoms, debris of decomposition.

The Latest

I am reliably informed that the universe is
ninety-six per cent dark matter; that scientists
will never know what dark matter is.

Haven't the godly heard this?
With ninety odd per cent of the universe to hide in,
God could be lolling on his massive elbow, observing
our scruffy four per cent and thinking,
'I really must tidy that up someday.'

In ninety-six per cent of the universe there's room
for any number of heavens, paradisi and hells,
not to mention the Valley of the Shining Hyacinth.

And you, my dead wife, could be stood in a room
in one of many mansions, working on a painting
and wondering why it's been so long since you saw me,
or your son, or daughter, not lost beneath
six feet of indifferent earth.

Inspiration

'Nothing left to write,'
I sometimes mutter
when inside my heart
seems empty as a shut
department store.

That my heart may close
its doors for ever, is,
as hippies used to say,
'A bit of a bummer,'
just what the doctor said
when you cried your cancer
was spreading everywhere.

She offered the latest pill
to 'sort the molecules
saddening your brain,'
so you'd forgive, forget,
the frisky little fuckers
friskily killing you.

And I wanted to kill her,
choke her with her pill-flogging pad.
though better, I realise,
alone in my loveless bed,
to have smashed her stupid mouth
to pulp, an unplastic-fixable
scarred mess that she'd have
to stare at the rest of her life
and have no choice but keep shut.

You never know what words wait
to barge their way into the store
of the written. Though sleep
shuffled close to silence them,
they shrugged it off, and thinking
it worth this bother, this risk
that at check-out they'd bag
only a bit of a bummer,
made me reach for my pad
and scribble this poem
sells nothing and no-one.

And now, putting down my pen,
I wonder what, if anything,
to make of this in the morning.

Blank

Desolate as this damp stump
in a mouldy creek,
indifferent to the brilliant white
of egret, I'm missing you again,
and running your memory
on a tape I fear will fade,
or corrode, into oblivion.

'The dead live in our memory,'
they say, forgetting that forgetting
wipes them blank. An easy chair,
an emptying bottle, the latest news –
who's screwing who, with cock
or cunning algorithm –
all these can kill again what time killed,
and just its passing, passing as I write,
(or don't, it matters not,) mean that,
in a decade or two, in six at very most,
not one among the teeming, dying billions,
will smile at memory of your smile,
or hear again what can't be caught in print,
on analogue, or digital, the kindness,
even of your laughing voice.

And what you meant to us, before transition
from earth to air, from voice to atom-dance –
useless to try to tell blank, busy posterity,
when, like a little fish gobbled up by egret,
your death will cause neither tear nor grimace,
and your memory, like this stump, like you,
will have rotted, and not a damp eye
in the house of the living to wish you back.

Sense

Not easy to live with, me,
so you upped sticks and left.
It seems that way sometimes
and guilt makes a sense
of the senseless. But, of course,
you didn't leave, weren't 'snatched
away' as I was going to say.
Rather, you were tugged, inch
by inch, terrified, to your death,
while organ, bone and flesh
were eaten away inside
by the cancer you were scared
would eat your face bit by bit.
It didn't. Death swallowed that whole.
The only sense is that it happened:
nothing makes sense of that.

Little Help

I photographed your face
to show that cancer
wasn't eating your jaw.
Not visibly, that is,
only scans and pain
could plot its progress.

It didn't work.
Nothing could tame
your terror that your face
would be eaten away.

Just how you felt,
no other can feel,
but you begged me
to take you to Zurich
for a final drink.

I couldn't.
Snapped that you could
book a plane on the net,
or swig the morphine
from the cupboard.

You didn't.

Shortly after,
cancer killed you.
Is anything left
of your face,
beneath wormy earth,
now six years gone?

Incident

Watching a beetle scurry
from stab of garden-fork
something longer, yellower,
blurs at edge of eye.

Carefully parting fat leaves
of the plant I am cheerfully
murdering, I see a frog, small,
which seems to look trustingly
though maybe just too cold to jump.

I spare its hide, hoping
to be repaid in munched-up slugs.

Much later that night, turning
off the too turn-offable match,
I think, could it have been Jackie?
After all, she spent long years teaching
Frog, and it's no dafter than the belief
that the dead sled back into our lives
on the back of falling pictures.

No dafter. But the tear that almost starts,
then decides to stay safe in its sac
is not for the chance you've grown amphibious,
cold, and a little repellent, but
that you haven't. That a frog is just a frog,
a slug a slug, a sheltering leaf a lucky chance
the fork stabbed an inch or two away.

Widowed

Thinking back, thinking forward,
to the pensioners we should have been,
bickering over trivia, fighting together
against your tumour, I remember
you said this Lyndhurst pony-snap
I'm looking at lacked composition.

Panting, weak from vile chemo,
you couldn't climb that sun-burnt,
one-tree hill, which I scurried up
and waved to you, then hurried back,
to capture this pot-bellied pony
on then new-fangled digital.

Later, you declared the snap OK,
pony and tiny hill combining
to triangulate picture-space.
That's how life goes, and yours
certainly, the only certainty among
wandering lacks of certainty, went.

And so, we couldn't cry out together,
this morning, at the green lizard halting
and jerking across the café's sun-fried patio,
while the old, grey coffee-drinkers shouted,
'Watch your feet! Don't squash the lizard!'
to new-comers with couple-cupped trays.

Life's Lovely Shimmer

Life's lovely shimmer
shimmers on river
of blood, mud and shit.

It's not unreal:
it gladdens the eye
and lightens the heart.

Like a baby making
its first steps, you can't
help loving it,

though that bright-
stepping baby walks
on a bed of millions
and millions of dead.

Worth Seeing

There are these two dots of girls
walk down my street, their blue school
blazers too big for them, and their legs so thin
you'd think they'd break. They always chatter,
and, today, one had a Santa cap, red
on her head. Though I hate December,
the month my wife died, the idiocies
of Christmas, no matter how depressed,
or bitter, I feel, when I see those two tots,
bold on the road of their lives, like wrens,
they are so tiny, my heart lifts, and I mind less
being old and ill and alone.

Reading *Modern Poetry in Translation*

Forced to endure another day
of my wife's ever-present absence,
my widowed morning wakes up badly
with a wide-awake, unshared lie-in,
cooking Sunday lunch a chore looming
and booming like a pub bore.
Later, bored past tears, I pick up MPT,
to pick on poems while the beef roasts.
Those forty minutes pass like one!
Refreshed by voices speak to me
despite the silence of their words,
by lives whose shape I glimpse and grasp
through shape-shifting, shape-presenting,
mist and sun-shaft of translation,
I cook the veg and carve the joint,
enjoy what's left of our family.

Evening Song

It's not too bad, this evening walk
beside a sleepy, sun-tanned river
where fish dim-flicker through shade
then flash in sun-drenched clarity.

Not too bad, though you stroll on your own,
and the cake and coffee in your bag
so loosely swung, in simulated
saunter, are for you alone.

Not too bad, though you guess at least one
of the sun-lit rooves the gulls squawk above,
hides a child sucking her father's knob
while mummy sips a Chardonnay.

We all know too much to be happy.
Even the sun, warm bath you're tempted
to lounge in, to watch the ducks bicker,
is dying, sure to burn up whatever's left,

by then, of people, planet (even space?).
Why then bother to recall, how thirty years
ago, you and your then young, then living,
wife, walked here? She was carrying

a small, diamond-patterned rug,
and some silly kid, perched in a tree
beside a bridge over this thin river,
threw a hard, green apple and hit

her on the head. She screamed, then laughed,
and wouldn't let you chase the little shit.
Nor did she drop the rug. You miss her.
If you could watch the solar system die,

would you miss it? Not all that much.
Sometimes, like now, it seems life's not too bad,
though not for those whose company is cruel.
But not too bad is very far from good.

After Treatment

I wanted to buy you
a little grey cardie
from Agnes B, size eight,
to fit you as neat, tight,
as I'd like to hold you now.
The costlier the better
to hint my sober love.

But you wouldn't even
enter the shop. You,
past haunter of sexy, Sixties,
Manchester boutiques,
whose white, Courreges boots
flaunted through the trailer
for the first film ever
about Lancaster University,
as if the director wanted to shout,
'New uni! No frumps here.'
you wouldn't enter.

I think you thought
you looked a fright.

Gift

'I found this,' the plumber grunts, holding out
something like a spoon, bent in the middle
to not quite a right-angle, 'Down in the drain.'
Puzzled, I take it, cold in my hand, its bowl
a claw, then grasp, it's a salad-server
bent by my long-dead wife to help her
unblock the drain, how many years ago?
At least eight. 'My wife bent that,' I try to boast,
hoping my voice will keep its bounce, not wail,
'Long before she died. She was never afraid
to get her hands dirty.' 'Sure,' he says,
'She was a genius. She's bent that to push it
round the bend. A very useful tool.'
Uncertain, I ask if he'd like to keep it,
and he's delighted, putting it in his bag.
'I'll use that a lot,' he smiles, 'Very good
for scooping stuff that's hiding round the bend.'

Since she died, I've mocked those widows' claims
that falling pictures are visits from their dead.
Now, a bent and chilly salad-server,
risen from a drain, brings back my wife,
kneeling, her manicured, picture-painting hands
deep in filthy water, scooping out muck.
Just for a moment, the plumber, who never
met her, and I, share the picture, a lovely
woman bent at the drain, digging down
with a thingy she's devised and bent
herself and a writing man watching.

Commotion

Voices outshout the wind,
there's crashing, splintering outside,
the booms of giant cranes at work,
waking me just past midnight,
getting me up. Feet hobbly with cramp.

The parted curtains show nothing
but dark street. The noises now
seem to have shifted round the back.
I push open the door of my son's
abandoned bedroom, and shout, shout.

A hooded man does something to the glass,
while between the window and me,
a shadow hunches. It turns and it's you!
In sudden clarity, smiling, stepping
forward as I ask, 'Where are we?'

Taking my hand in yours, you say,
'My darling,' cliché that alive
you would disdain, and all the world
warms gold and new as, closer still,
you fold your arms around my back.

And then I wake, alone in bed,
wondering where we've been. Wondering
too, months later, why it means so much,
the best of all that's happened in these,
our widowed years.

Today

Today, I drove to see
a friend's painting,

passed a big, bold hill
I guess is millions old,

its green more vibrant
than kingfisher blue,

and though sun shone as hardly
ever, and my car thrilled too,

beneath all that welcome light
a dark river of missing you,

how you loved trips out to shows,
how vibrant paint lit you.

Stairs

Stairs we climbed to passion in our bed,
stairs we dawdled up to doze, ablute,
stairs we scampered down to rush to work,
stairs that bore our toddlers' tiny shoes,
their burgeoning to teenage trainers priced
near gold, stairs as much a part of every day
as bickering, or socks, or jokes at tea,
and as taken-for-granted, like life itself,
stairs where, legs gone, you fell on the first step,
first step to ten days dying in our bed,
stairs which, like lounge, kitchen, garden,
painting-table, books, you never saw again,
stairs they carried you down, in body-bag,
stairs I fell down, drunk with drink and grief,
stairs my grandson jumps from, giggling,
into his mother's gentle clutch, oblivious
to their thirty years of bearing us up
and letting us down, a snakes and ladders
you're no longer part of, our game boxed-up,
your counter no longer counting, his
hardly begun to know that it's in play.

Those Little Acts

By Frink's striding Christ,
beneath Salisbury spire,
I put my arm around
your boney shoulder,
cancer eating your flesh,
and said, 'I love you.'

You skipped. For joy,
or surprise? I don't know,
but there was a foot
of air beneath your feet.
It matters not,
cynics would sneer,
near twenty years later
and you long dead.

But it does.
That little leap may lift
a lonely life, though spire
fall and statue shatter,
and even your cancer
is gone with that day.

Acknowledgements

Thanks are due to the editors of the following publications, where some of these poems were first published – *Acumen, The Interpreter's House, Tears in the Fence* and *Seven* (Impulse Press).